Easter Remembered

Easter Remembered

Reflections in Poetry and Prose

María Alvarez

The Hermit Kingdom Press
Cheltenham ♦ Seoul ♦ Bangalore ♦ Cebu

**EASTER REMEMBERED:
REFLECTIONS IN POETRY AND PROSE**

Copyright © 2005 by Maria Alvarez

All rights reserved. No part of this book may be reproduced in any form or by any means, electronic or mechanical, including photocopying, recording, or by any information storage and retrieval system, without permission in writing from the publisher.

ISBN 1-59689-012-6

(USA) Library of Congress Control Number: 2005920541

Write-To Address:

The Hermit Kingdom Press
3741 Walnut Street, Suite 407
Philadelphia, PA 19104
United States of America

Info@TheHermitKingdomPress.com

Hermit Kingdom
12 South Bridge, Suite 370
Edinburgh, EH1 1DD
Scotland

http://www.TheHermitKingdomPress.com

For Latino Christians
In the United States
Who love Jesus Christ

"Somewhere and somehow these people are never going to be the same. It's very important to us that people question, that they participate and that they are never afraid to have some principle and stand by that principle."

Cesar Chavez
American Labor Leader
(1927-1993)

Contents

What Easter Means To Me <17>
(Testimony 1)

"Rejected" <34>

"Serve and Served" <35>

"Cursed Jews" <36>

"The Jewish Mob" <37>

"Jewish Political Leaders" <38>

"Jewish Religious Leaders" <39>

"The Law Breaker" <40>

"Jesus' Followers" <41>

"Laws" <42>

"Clever Jews" <43>

"God-Man" <44>

"Suffering" <45>

What Easter Means for the Suffering <46>
(Testimony 2)

"Triumphal Entry" <56>

"Where Are My Disciples?" <57>

"The Betrayer" <58>

"Pierced" <60>

"Crown of Thorns" <61>

"It Could Have Been Different" <62>

"Hung up to Dry" <63>

What Easter Means for the Future <64>
(Testimony 3)

"Joy of Easter" <76>

"Jesus Is Arisen!" <77>

"Death Not Be Proud" <78>

"Master of Life" <80>

"The Resurrection" <81>

"Life Source" <82>

"Give Me Life" <83>

"Future Hope" <84>

"Jesus Is My God" <85>

"Divine Power" <86>

"The Judge" <87>

"The Disciples" <88>

"The Women" <89>

"Glory" <90>

Easter Remembered

Easter Remembered

What Easter Means To Me

Easter may mean a lot of different things for many people. When some people think about Easter, they may think about Easter egg hunts and all the festivities attached to the Christian holiday.

Some may think about the new clothing they receive in Easter for the great Easter Sunday worship service. There had been a period in American history in which the only time some children received new clothing was on Easter.

Others may think about all the nice chocolates during Easter time. There seems to be reincarnation of chocolates in ways that it did not seem possible. Egg-shaped chocolates and fuzzy bunny chocolates color the grocery store in bright yellow, red, and green wrappers.

For your Korean Christian neighbor, Easter may mean waking up really early in the morning and going to the Easter Sunday Morning Prayer sponsored by all the Korean Christian churches in the city. Philadelphia's Korean Christians have traditionally met for Easter morning prayers on the steps of the

Easter Remembered

Philadelphia Art Museum, where Rocky has the famous scene in the movie with the catchy jingle tune.

For me, Easter conjures up images not so much of happiness and celebration, but rather about suffering. I do not think of Easter in terms of Christians gathering to pray in the morning, but rather in terms of Jesus Christ who was resurrected from death to an empty tomb – an evidence of the desertion of all His disciples at the last hour of His death on the cross.

Easter for me, therefore, is about the suffering of Jesus Christ. Even Christ's resurrection highlights in contrast the tremendous suffering and betrayal He experienced.

I know that there will be those out there who want to just celebrate happiness and joy when thinking about Easter. But for me, celebrating the resurrection has little meaning apart from remembering the suffering and death of Christ.

It is in this vein, I have written the poems in this book. I find the true meaning of Easter in the suffering and death of Jesus Christ. The resurrection of Christ has meaning only when seen in the context of the background.

Easter Remembered

I would like to ponder the relationship between the resurrecttion and suffering of Christ a bit further.

What does it mean for Christ to be resurrected from death? It means that Christ has defeated death. How can we think about the victory of Christ in resurrection apart from the fact of the death of Christ? It is impossible.

To think about the death of Christ is crucial to Christian understanding of Easter. And as a Christian, I would like to focus on the true meaning of Easter.

And to think about the death of Christ is to study the way Jesus Christ died and the factors that led to His earthly demise.

What can we know about the suffering and death of Jesus Christ? I would say that two words describe the suffering and death of Jesus Christ: deception and corruption.

I will unpack the two words in greater details. What role did deception play in the suffering and death of Jesus Christ?

Jewish leaders deceived Jesus Christ into thinking that they were interested in His teaching. The New Testament clearly shows that Jewish leaders followed Jesus Christ around to find a way to have Jesus Christ arrested and killed.

Jewish leaders purposely asked tricky question and tried to see how Jesus Christ would respond. Jewish leaders hoped that Jesus Christ would say things that were politically incorrect. Jewish leaders were hoping that Jesus would say things that would give them information to entrap Him. Jewish leaders wished that Jesus would alienate His disciples and the people by what He said.

There was certainly deception involved. Jewish leaders pretended to befriend Jesus Christ when, in fact, they were interested in minimizing His influence and effecttiveness. Jewish leaders wanted to make Jesus Christ into a lame duck who could not function in His setting. Jewish leaders wanted Jesus to have no legs to stand on. Thus, with this surreptitious goal in mind Jewish leaders followed Jesus Christ around.

Jesus Christ saw through the deception of the Jewish leaders, pretending to be His followers, interested in His teaching. Jesus Christ often criticized the many hours that Jewish leaders prayed.

Jesus knew their hearts even if others only believed what they saw.

Jesus knew that the holiness that Jewish leaders exhibited in public concealed the evil intent in their hearts. Jesus knew that Jewish leaders could keep all the Jewish laws and the laws of the land, while making themselves into enemies of God. God sees the heart and not merely the outside.

Jewish leaders were not only practicing deception themselves. They wanted to recruit people to practice deception against Jesus Christ.

The New Testament shows that Jews tried to produce false witnesses against Jesus in order to get Jesus Christ arrested and killed. Jewish leaders knew that they had to induce evidence, to incite Jesus into error.

Jewish leaders knew that they needed witnesses to convict Jesus. The problem was that these witnesses knew about the work of incitement that Jewish leaders engaged in to have Jesus Christ arrested.

The only way that Jewish leaders could successfully have Jesus Christ arrested without implicating themselves was to have witnesses participate in deception. The witnesses had to tell that Jesus Christ was evil and the Jewish leaders were good. Jewish leaders, according to the New Testament, tried to produce false witnesses.

There were other ways that Jewish leaders tried to encourage others to participate in deception. Jewish leaders sometimes paid cold, hard cash.

The most visible case in the Bible is the buying of Judas Iscariot. Jewish leaders paid Judas Iscariot hard cash to betray Jesus Christ.

What was the nature of the betrayal? It was deception. Jewish leaders were paying Judas Iscariot to participate in their deception. They were in fact saying, "Why don't you pretend to follow Jesus Christ, but betray Him?" They obviously believed that everyone had their price.

In the case of Judas Iscariot, they were right. Jewish leaders were able to pay Judas Iscariot to participate in their deception. Judas continued to follow Jesus Christ, pretending to be a true follower.

This makes you think about today. How many people pretend to be a Christian while practicing the deception of Jewish leaders? If

Easter Remembered

Judas Iscariot was able to carry out the deception until the death of Jesus Christ, you can believe that there are present leaders in the Christian church who practice deception successfully.

When you think about it, Judas Iscariot as one of the 12 disciples of Jesus Christ is equivalent to the Archibishop in the Roman Catholic Church. Is there an Archbiship or two today who are practicing deception? Are there Christian ministers who pretend to follow Jesus Christ but all the while participating in the deception of Jewish leaders?

Days leading up to the death of Jesus Christ particularly saw heightening of the deception both by Jewish leaders and those whom Jewish leaders recruited against Jesus Christ. It is impossible to talk about the suffering and death of Jesus Christ without thinking about the deception against Jesus Christ.

Besides deception, another word comes to mind when thinking about the suffering and death of Jesus Christ. That word is corruption.

There was much corruption surrounding the suffering and death of Jesus. The fact that they were able to arrest Jesus Christ is a testimony to the corruption of the system.

What was Jesus Christ doing but preaching the Word of God? He was free to expound the Bible like anyone else. But Jewish leaders did not like what Jesus had to say. Jesus Christ's teachings directly contradicted the teachings of the Jewish leaders of the time.

Jewish leaders taught that Jewish laws must be kept for one to be saved and to know God. Jesus Christ taught that Jewish laws were not important at all for coming to know God.

Not only did Jesus attack Jewish laws with words but with His actions. Jesus defended His disciples picking the heads of grain on Sabbath Day. Rigid Jewish laws considered this as work. Jesus showed how ridiculous Jewish laws were.

Jesus also attacked Jewish laws on purity. Jewish laws were becoming ridiculous in emphasizing washing rituals and bathing to give people their worth. Jesus attacked the laws constructed in a ridiculous way to draw nearer to God. Jesus showed that it was not in the ritual bathing that people developed relationship with God. Rather, Jesus showed that the heart had to be pure and that faith should be placed in Him.

Jewish leaders did not like the fact that Jesus Christ directly attacked their teachings. Jewish leaders had a vested interest in emphasizing their rituals and laws because it was a way for them to gain influence in society and be seen as important. Jewish leaders did not like Jesus Christ showing the people that their way of doing things was wrong and offends God.

Jewish leaders felt their authority and popularity threatened by what Jesus Christ said and did, so they corrupted the system in order to imprison Jesus Christ and have Him killed.

The New Testament account of the trial of Jesus Christ in the Jewish courts shows how corrupt the judiciary system was. In fact, in the Gospel of John, there is an account of Jewish leaders plotting in the Jewish court to have Jesus Christ arrested and then killed.

So, when Jesus Christ is actually brought to trial in the Jewish court, we know that he was seen as guilty by Jewish judges even before He entered the courtroom. Furthermore, we know that Jews have decided to have Jesus Christ killed even before He set foot in the room of the Sanhedrin.

This is clearly a corruption of the judicial system. There was a court decision to get Christ killed by judiciary system and Jewish leaders carried out their evil plan, while keeping the appearances that Jesus was actually under trial.

It was really no trial. It was a lynching session. The whole trial in the Sanhedrin was a show by Jewish leaders to pat themselves on the back. They knew that they were there to lynch Jesus Christ. That was the whole point. They just gave the semblance of justice to make themselves look good.

It was a sick way of taking pleasure in a corrupt judiciary system. It was a twisted way of getting kicks out of an innocent person.

Jesus Christ taught the Word of God. There was no law against His freedom of speech. All that He taught – even calling Jews "children of the devil" – were all perfectly legal. Jesus had the right to freedom of speech under the laws of the Roman Empire.

Jewish leaders just did not like the fact that Jesus attacked

Judaism and Jewish leaders. Thus, they corrupted the system.

The death sentence against Jesus Christ was passed at the highest Jewish court in Jerusalem. But the Jewish leaders were not content with the decision of the Sanhedrin. Jewish leaders wanted the Roman court to pass the death penalty against Jesus Christ.

Thus, having corrupted the Jewish legal system, Jewish leaders sought to corrupt the Roman legal system. How did Jewish leaders go about their systematic program of corruption?

There was lobbying at the top. Jewish religious leaders and political figures tried to get Roman representatives to send Jesus to His death by trying to portray Jesus Christ as a traitor to the Roman Empire.

Jewish leaders whispered in the ears of Pilate and other Roman representatives that Jesus must die because He is upsetting peace and order in the country. Jewish leaders tried to paint Jesus Christ as breaking the laws of the Roman Empire. Jewish leaders pushed to portray Jesus Christ as dangerous to society.

Jewish leaders were corrupting the justice system of the Roman Empire for their own ends. Jewish leaders did not like Jesus Christ and what He taught, so Jewish leaders lobbied at the highest levels of government to influence their decisions against Jesus Christ.

But Jewish leaders were not only involved in corrupting the official representatives of the Roman Empire's government in Palestine. Jewish leaders corrupted the legal process by mobilizing the mob against Jesus Christ.

Jewish leaders painted Jesus Christ as evil and unethical. Jewish leaders tried to portray Jesus as a breaker of laws and hater of Judaism. Jewish leaders incited the Jewish masses to participate in the killing of Jesus Christ. The Jewish masses were spurred on to shout, "Crucify Him! Crucify Him!"

The New Testament is clear in showing that Jewish leaders were successful in convincing ordinary Jews in the street that Jesus Christ must die. The guilt was assumed. Ordinary Jews were to do what they could to get Jesus Christ convicted and killed.

Indeed, Jewish leaders coruptted the system from top down.

Official government officials were coaxed into passing a guilty verdict against Jesus Christ. Ordinary people in the street were encouraged to oppose Jesus Christ and even verbally abuse Him and to create a popular disorder against Him.

The corruption of the system of justice and society was thorough from top down. And it was a systematic program by Jewish leaders. The New Testament is clear on this point.

So, the Bible is emphatic in declaring Jewish leaders as instigators of deception and corruption for the purpose of killing Jesus Christ. The Bible is clear in showing ordinary Jews as guilty in participating actively in the corrupted system to have Jesus Christ killed.

The New Testament portrays all this as the fulfilment of Old Testament prophecies against the Jews. And the New Testament shows in all this the rejection of Jews as the people of God.

True heirs of Abraham's faith are those who accept Jesus Christ as God and put their faith in Him as the Savior. Christians are the true people of God. Jews have been abandoned. Killing of Jesus Christ through deception and corruption was the final straw.

And the New Testament shows how Jesus Christ suffered. Jesus Christ suffered all kinds of humiliation, pain, and anguish as the result of deception and corruption.

In the days leading to Easter Sunday, the suffering intensified. And as Jesus suffered, His earthly friends fell away, one by one.

Some of Jesus' earthly friends disappeared from the scene because they were truly afraid. They thought to themselves that if Jewish leaders were powerful enough to kill someone like Jesus Christ, then they could easily kill them. So, they went into a kind of hiding.

Some of the earthly friends disappeared because they were enticed by earthly wealth. Jesus was being arrested by police and was being dragged through a corrupt legal system. It was becoming obvious that there was no wealth to be had following Jesus Christ. They turned their backs on Jesus and went towards earthly riches.

Others fell away from Jesus Christ because they were too deceived. Jewish leaders successfully convinced them that Jesus

Christ was evil. They persuaded Jesus Christ's former friends that opposing Jesus Christ was the ethical thing to do. Jesus Christ is a hater of Judaism and Jewish laws. How could you not oppose Him?

Perhaps, the enemies of Christ pointed to all the curses Jesus Christ uttered against the Jews. Jesus Christ called the Jews, "children of the devil." And there were other curses uttered against the Jews. Also, Jesus acted in a violent way in the Temple, overturning moneychangers' tables and wreaking havoc. Jewish leaders successfully portrayed Jesus Christ as rude, savage, violent, and a person lacking good character.

Thus, some were deceived by Jewish leaders and fell away from Jesus Christ.

Jesus Christ's pain at the hand of a corrupted police and unfair justice system, therefore, was compounded by the betrayal of His friends. At the center of all the corruption and deception were Jewish leaders who wanted Jesus Christ killed.

When I think about Easter, I cannot ignore the suffering and pain of Jesus Christ. When I think about Easter, I cannot overlook the deception and corruption perpetrated against Jesus Christ with intentionality and efficiency. When I think about Easter, I cannot forget the Jewish purpose to have Jesus Christ killed. The Bible does not want us to forget and that is why all four Gospels record the deception and corruption of Jews in having Jesus Christ killed. The Bible wants us to remember for all eternity.

For me, it is impossible to think about Easter Sunday without thinking about the suffering and death of Jesus Christ. Without thinking seriously about Jesus Christ's suffering and death, it is impossible to truly appreciate the greatness of the resurrection and of Easter Sunday.

For me, Easter is meaningless without the suffering and death of Christ. It is in the suffering of Christ that we find Jesus Christ's love and humanity. It is in the death of Jesus Christ that we understand the love of God. Easter and resurrection of Jesus Christ shows us that the suffering and death was done for our benefit and on our behalf. The victory of Easter shows that the King of kings and the LORD of lords, Jesus Christ, who reigns supreme as God understands

Easter Remembered

human suffering, injustice, and sickness. It is this God who understands who is triumphant over death and suffering. It is this God who can lead Christians toward life everlasting.

As a Christian, that is a very comforting thought. Jesus paid it all, and all to Him, I owe. Jesus Christ has conquered sin and has forgiven me. It is in the presence of Jesus Christ that I, as a Christian, can live life eternal.

Easter is about the suffering, death, and resurrection of my God, who took on human flesh to save me and give me eternal life. And it is in the spirit of thankfulness for the love of Christ Jesus that I write my poems in this book to celebrate Easter.

Easter Remembered

"Rejected"

The chosen people
They say they are
But they rejected me,
The promised Messiah.

Jesus is my name
And Christ is my title.
I am the one the prophets of Old
Foretold and looked forward to.

Rejected,
I was.
Despising me,
They spat on me.

The so-called chosen people
Treated me like a criminal,
Informing me to the police.
With violence, they attacked me.

For the people
Who should have received me,
I was nothing more
Than their punching bag.

Rejected,
Despised,
I was put to the cross
By Jews hating me.

Easter Remembered

"Serve and Served"

I served the people
To help them to salvation,
To know God.
But they would not be served.

They would not be served
With God's love,
Salvation through me,
The Holy One promised.

They would not be served
With the message of the New
Testament to lock the door
That would lead to destruction.

Instead, they served me
With an arrest warrant
To have me crucified.
They were Jews who informed.

Easter Remembered

"Cursed Jews"

Jews are cursed
Because they had
Christ put to death.
Jews manipulated the police,
The justice system,
And political power.

Jews are cursed
Because they were blind
To the message of salvation
From Jesus Christ the Lord,
The God of the Bible
Who appeared before them.

Jews are cursed
Because they spat on Christ,
Followed Him everywhere
In order to cause His fall,
And ultimately
Jews had Christ killed.

Easter Remembered

"The Jewish Mob"

The Jewish mob
Pursued Jesus
In order to kill Him.

The Jewish mob
Followed Jesus around
Without faith.

The Jewish mob
Mocked Jesus
And laughed at Him.

The Jewish mob
Relished the suffering
Of the Messiah.

The Jewish mob
Stood by
As Jewish leaders persecuted Jesus.

The Jewish mob
Cried,
Crucify Him! Crucify Him!

The Jewish mob
Smiled
As Jesus died on the cross.

Easter Remembered

"Jewish Political Leaders"

I am a Jewish leader,
Entered politics
To advance
Jewish causes.

Jewish political leader,
Am I.
And Christ must
Die.

Christ is a threat
To Jewish causes.
Christ' Gospel
Is a curse for Judaism.

I hold political power
As a Jew
For a reason –
To advance Jewish interests.

For Jewish interest
Must Christ
The so-called Son of God
Must die.

Easter Remembered

"Jewish Religious Leaders"

I am a Jewish religious leader
And I hate Jesus
Who is soft
On Judaism.

Soft he is,
This one called Christ.
Does he keep the Sabbath?
No!

Soft Jesus is on Judaism
And disrespectful
To all things Jewish.
The soft one must perish!

I am a Jewish religious leader,
And I will see to the death of Jesus.
Jesus is a threat to Judaism,
And Jesus must die.

I am a Jewish religious leader,
And I see killing Christ
As my mission
Because I am a leader of Judaism.

Easter Remembered

"The Law Breaker"

Jesus is a law breaker.
Jesus breaks Jewish laws.
How evil He is,
The law breaker.

I am a Jew,
Who keeps the law.
I respect Judaism
And teachings of rabbis.

Jesus is a law breaker,
Plain and simple.
Jesus flaunts in Jewish faces
His disdain for Jewish laws.

As a Jew
Who respects the law,
I hate Jesus Christ,
The law breaker.

Jesus should be put into jail
For His disregard for Jews
And the laws protecting Jews
And Jewish interest.

Easter Remembered

"Jesus' Followers"

What can the followers of Jesus do
When we Jews put Him to death?
We are organized and powerful.
They are weak and soft.

What can the disciples of Jesus do
When we Jews arrest Jesus
And put Him in chains?
Jesus' disciples are scary-cats.

What can the Christians do
When we Jews persecute Jesus?
They have no political power
Because we have the control

What can the believers of Jesus do
When we Jews crucify Jesus?
We control the police
And have influence over justice.

What can the followers of Jesus do
When we Jews kill Jesus?
They will just have to sit and watch.
Christians are helpless to protect.

Easter Remembered

"Laws"

We Jews control the laws
Of this land where we live.
We Jews control
The keepers of the laws.

We Jews control
The enforcers of the laws.
We Jews control
The makers of the laws.

Laws belong to us,
The Jews.
Who can oppose us,
The puppet-masters of laws?

They are helpless to protect Jesus
Because we Jews control the laws
In this land that we live.
And legally Jesus must die.

Easter Remembered

"Clever Jews"

Call us clever Jews
Because we control the system.
We can have Jesus followed.
We can put props in place.

Call us clever Jews
Because we know how to trap.
We put snares everywhere
To capture Jesus at His words.

Call us clever Jews –
We are manipulation experts.
We know how to trick people
Into doing things to harm Jesus.

Call us clever Jews
Because we can get Him killed.
Jesus has no chance
But die in Jewish hands.

Call us clever Jews
Because we can get away with it.
Who will bring us Jews to justice
After we kill the maniac prophet?

Easter Remembered

"God-Man"

Jesus Christ is God-Man –
100% God,
100% human,
But without the sin.

Jesus Christ is Yahweh –
God who acts in the Old Testament.
He is the Creator God,
Of the same essence.

Jesus Christ is God –
Infinite and eternal
Living Word
As John testifies.

Jesus Christ is Man –
God took on human flesh
In order to have a body
To sacrifice for our sins.

Jesus Christ is God-Man,
Who is the Savior of the world.
Jesus Christ will give salvation
To all who want it.

Easter Remembered

"Suffering"

Jesus Christ knew suffering.
Nowhere could He call home
On earth as He wandered
From place to place.

Without luxuries of the world
Living a simple life
Jesus crusaded
To save humankind.

With a human body
Jesus Christ knew hunger.
He experienced
Harsh weather in the open.

Jesus Christ preached salvation,
But Jewish leaders persecuted Him
Psychologically and verbally,
And even by the use of laws.

Jesus Christ knew suffering.
Far and wide people knew
That Jesus Christ gave up all
To preach the message of salvation.

What Easter Means for the Suffering

There are a lot of people who suffer in the world. People suffer from all kinds of causes. Those who suffer do not have many channels of comfort.

For the people who suffer, Easter can be one important reality in their life that can provide real comfort. Easter is significant for the suffering.

Easter has been important for the suffering in the past. Easter continues to be a valuable source of comfort for the suffering. Easter will be a significant comfort source for the future for the suffering.

There are many accounts in Christianity about the value of Easter for the suffering. History of Christianity is filled with martyrdom. It is difficult to study the history of Christianity in any land without coming across martyrdom.

The most deeply moving account of martyrdom was one I heard in a sermon. There was a group of American male missionaries who went to the Philippines, to a region where head-hunters and cannibals lived.

Easter Remembered

They were young men who desired to share the joy of Easter with the cannibals. The young American missionaries went, armed only with the Bible and the love of Jesus Christ.

They were idealistic to be sure. They were hoping that the message of the Christian Gospel would be accepted readily and that the cannibals' lives would be enriched spiritually as the result of the Good News.

But these men were not idiots. They knew that they were approaching people who have never heard of Jesus Christ. They knew also that the cannibals ate human beings. They knew that there was a high probability that they would be killed and eaten.

Despite the recognition of the dangers, Christian missionaries from the United States went into the most dangerous areas of the Philippines. The Philippine government discouraged them. The American government told them that they could not protect them. They still went, grabbing onto the hope of Easter.

In their ears rang the words of Jesus Christ: "I am the resurrecttion and the life. Those who abide in me will live forever." They knew the

Easter Remembered

promise of the resurrected Lord God Jesus Christ to be true.

And the expected happened. As soon as the young American Christian missionaries arrived in cannibal land, they were captured. Before they could say anything about Jesus Christ, they were killed. And they were eaten by the cannibals.

The news of their death reached their wives, who were praying for them. They were dedicated to Jesus Christ like their husbands and shared the same Christian vision.

Instead of wailing and bemoaning the death of their beloved husbands, who died so young, the young wives of American Christian missionaries prayed together to seek the will of Jesus Christ.

Unanimously, they resolved to go to the same area their husbands had gone to share the Christian Gospel. They decided that they will bring the Christian Gospel so that they will have the opportunity of receiving Easter joy and comfort.

Of course, they knew that there was a good possibility that they, too, would be killed. After all, their husbands had been killed and eaten by the same people. Surely, they were afraid. Who would not be under the circumstances?

But they went – all the wives of the Christian missionaries who were eaten by cannibals. They, too, went, only armed with the Bible and the love of Jesus Christ. They were eager to share the joy of Easter, grounded in the message of the Resurrection.

"I am the way and the life. Those who come to me will never thirst but have everlasting life."

They heard the Easter promise of Jesus Christ and boldly went, despite human fears and sadness arising from their great loss.

This time, the unexpected happened. The cannibals did not kill them. They did not eat them.

There was a long standing tradition among the cannibals there that they not kill women nor eat them. Of course, the dead missionaries' wives did not know of the tradition. As far as they were concerned, there was high probability that they, too, would be killed and eaten.

The women of faith went in faith in Jesus Christ and in the hope of Easter Resurrection.

It was the plan of Jesus Christ to work through these women

Easter Remembered

of faith. They worked among the cannibals, eventually being able to communicate with them.

One by one, cannibals came to accept Jesus Christ as their personal Lord God and Savior. Eventually, the whole cannibal village became Christians. They gave up their cannibalism. Eventually, they became one of the model villages in the Philippines.

For the missionaries and their wives, they were able to hang onto the joy and comfort of Easter during their suffering. When faced with martyrdom, they held fast onto the hope of Resurrection.

There are many other accounts of martyrdom in Christian history. There are perhaps too many to mention in such a short space. I think it is absolutely beneficial to read accounts of Christian martyrdom throughout history.

For my part, I would like to share one other significant account of martyrdom. Perhaps, it is because I am a woman that I would like to share this particular events of Christian martyrdom.

During the early centuries of Christian history, there were some horrific accounts of Christian martyrdom, particularly targeted against women.

Perhaps, there was greater resentment when women became Christians in some areas because it offended male pride and sensibilities in the land. Maybe the people in the area felt their way of life was fundamentally endangered by women becoming Christians.

For whatever reason, in some areas, women suffered horrific Christian martyrdom. One memorable area was in the area of Iraq and Iran in the first few centuries of the Christian era.

There were women who became Christians, and they were tortured in horrible ways. One woman who became a Christian in the area of Iran over a thousand years ago was cut, piece by piece. She refused to give up her faith in Jesus Christ, steadfastly holding onto the hope of Easter and putting faith in the promise of Resurrection unto eternal life. She died a slow, very painful death.

There were quite a number of Christian women in the area at that time who suffered tremendously and suffered martyrdom in the most hideous fashion.

They were able to endure such great suffering and pain because they had faith in Jesus Christ and hope in the joy and comfort of Easter.

Easter has played an important role in the thousands of years of Christian history in giving comfort to those facing and suffering martyrdom for their Christian faith.

Easter did not only provide comfort and hope in the midst of extreme suffering, torture, and death. The reality of Easter often served to encourage poor people and people suffering from the daily grind and ill fortunes of society.

Throughout the history of Christianity, many people found life sweet and comforting because they realized the meaning of Easter and its consequences for them personally.

Yes, they were poor and suffering on this earth, but after death, they will be raised to life by Jesus Christ, who will lead them toward eternal life in Heaven to reign with Him forever. With the knowledge in the hope of Easter and the promise of Resurrection many poor who were Christians found joy in life and meaning in their existence.

Easter Remembered

When Karl Marx said that religion was the opium of the masses, he was speaking as a leftist intellectual, who really did not know what being poor was. Marx did not know what it meant to suffer in a society as an outcast or dejected through ill fortune. Marx lived as an intellectual, wrote as an intellectual, and died as an intellectual.

It is no surprise today that Communism has so utterly failed. The worse crime of Communism, in my opinion, was illegalizing Christianity. Marxism deprived people, especially the oppressed people, of the hope of Easter and the promise of Resurrection. That is more evil than any other violations that Communist regimes have committed.

Many poor and oppressed people in history have found comfort in life through Easter and the promise of Resurrection. And many people continue to find comfort in the message of Easter.

Jesus Christ had said, "Store up treasures in Heaven where rust and decay do not destroy. Don't store up treasures on earth." Jesus Christ encouraged His followers two thousand years ago to look Heavenward and not down towards the earth.

Easter Remembered

Jesus Christ's encouragement was to hold onto the hope that is far greater than anything this world could offer. The promise was real. The resurrection of the dead was real. The Kingdom of Heaven where the poor and oppressed will enter to rule forever with Christ was real. This was the message of Jesus Christ. This is the hope of Easter.

Just as Jesus Christ rose from death, He would raise the faithful from death in order that they might live eternal life in Easter joy with Christ, the King of kings and the LORD of lords.

For many throughout history and today, the promise of Easter joy is the greatest hope that they have in life.

The hope is real, more real for many than the earthly love passed on from parents to their children. Easter hope keeps many people going and living with contentment.

Easter is a true source of comfort to those who believe in Jesus Christ as God and Savior.

Christians are convinced beyond the shadow of doubt that Jesus Christ will come back in the end of days to judge the quick and the dead.

Those who have been faithful to Jesus Christ will be raised from death to live in eternal happiness, forever and ever. Eternity of happiness far outweighs even up to 110 years of extreme suffering.

Easter is very significant for the suffering and the oppressed. Easter can be a religious value and a personal value for those who have true faith in Jesus Christ, the Creator God of the world.

Easter Remembered

"Triumphal Entry"

Jesus entered Jerusalem
Like a king,
As prophesied in the Bible.
Jesus Christ is the universal king.

But the triumphal entry harbingered
The coming of the Kingdom rule
In the Second Coming.
Jesus will return in the future.

In the days leading up to His death,
Jesus' triumphal entry gave hope.
But He was to meet His death
At the hands of unrighteous ones.

Riding like a king into Jerusalem
Showed in contrast the cross.
The rejection of the King by Jews
Testified in the Christ crucified.

The triumphal entry condemns Jews
Who should have accepted Him.
Jews refused and tortured Him.
Christ ended up dead on the cross.

Easter Remembered

"Where Are My Disciples?"

As Jesus hung on the tree
Death staring Him on the face,
He looked around,
All around.

Here and there,
Jesus looked
To see a glimpse
Of all the disciples He loved.

They had run away,
All of them,
At the very hour
When Jesus needed them most.

At the hour of His death,
His disciples were invisible.
They were in hiding,
Fearful that they too would be killed.

In the field of death
As Jesus hung to die,
Weight of blood closing His eyes,
Jesus saw not his disciples.

Empty,
Bleak,
Missing
Were Jesus' disciples.

Easter Remembered

"The Betrayer"

What went through the mind
Of the betrayer of Judas
As he accepted silver
For the life of Jesus?

Was it jealousy for Jesus' fame
That compelled him to do his deed?
Did he covet Jesus' powers?
Why did the betrayer sell Jesus out?

What went through the mind
Of the betrayer Judas
As he shook hands with evil ones
And plotted against Jesus' life?

Did the betrayer feel closer to evil
Than to the one chosen to do good?
Evil had power and control over laws;
That was visible and appeared real.

What went through the mind
Of the betrayer Judas
As he anticipated the death of Jesus,
The teacher who taught him all?

Was it wanting to belong to the elite
That caused him to compromise
Himself and all that he had learned?
Was fame worth it all?

Easter Remembered

What went through the mind
Of the betrayer Judas
As he understood that Jesus
Will die because of his actions?

All sense of right and wrong slipped
As the betrayer became blinded
By his own desires
And selfish gains.

What went through the mind
Of the betrayer Judas
When he saw Jesus arrested
On his cue?

Did he not feel a pang of guilt
That he had betrayed himself as
He betrayed God's Chosen?
The betrayer Judas killed himself.

Easter Remembered

"Pierced"

Christ's hands were
Pierced,
With the rudeness
Of disbelief.

Nails were hammered in
By unbelievers
Refusing to believe
That Jesus is God.

Christ's feet were
Pierced,
With the evil intent
Of the conniving ones.

Haters of Christ
Colluded in secret
To have nails
Driven into Christ's feet.

Christ's side was
Pierced,
With the betrayal
Of those who purported to follow.

A spear was driven in
To the side of Jesus
Who suffered physical pain
And the pain of betrayal.

Easter Remembered

"Crown of Thorns"

Crown of thorns
Hung on the head of Christ.
Nay, it was imbedded
Painfully like a piercing nail
On the delicate head of Christ.

The blood flowed
From the pierced pores,
Trickling down
Christ's peaceful face,
Strained under suffering.

It was a crown of mockery
For the innocent preacher
Who proclaimed
The coming of the Kingdom of God,
Being led towards an unjust death.

Crown of thorns
Rested visibly on His head –
Blood-stained,
Jagged,
Embodiment of death.

Easter Remembered

"It Could Have Been Different"

It could have been different
If Jews accepted Christ.
It could have meant
A world of difference.

But Jews rejected Jesus.
Teachers of the law
Colluded with Jewish leaders
To have Christ killed on the cross.

It could have been different
If Jewish leaders
Tolerated the difference
That Christ represented.

Intolerant,
Jewish leaders instigated the mob
To have Christ killed
Under the veil of law and order.

It could have been different
If Jewish masses refused
To follow the order of
The Jewish elites.

2000 years of Jewish suffering –
Is it due to karma?
What goes around comes around?
What a tragedy!

Easter Remembered

"Hung up to Dry"

Christ was hung up to dry
By a band of ruffians
In respectable clothing
And proper titles.

Christ came first to Jews
They say
But it was the Jews
Who did not want Him.

It was the Jews with titles,
Respect in society,
Teachers of the law,
Those with wealth and power,

Who wanted Christ out of the way.
Was Christ a threat
To Jewish sense of security?
Did they think, without Christ

They could succeed?
In 70 AD
Jerusalem was completely ruined
And all Jews kicked out for millennia.

Little did killing Jesus do
To help Jews.
Perhaps injustice hastened
The end of Jews in Jerusalem.

What Easter Means for the Future

Easter is not a mere abstraction. It is not a fictional myth in the past that has no relevance for the future. Rather, Easter is a real historical phenomenon with important consequences and implications for the future. Easter can be a symbol of hope and renewal.

Jesus Christ was raised from death after being nailed to death on the cross. His death was real. His resurrection from death was real.

In the resurrection, Jesus Christ proved that He is God. Jesus Christ is the God of the Old Testament (referred to as Yahweh), and He is the God of the New Testament. The resurrection conclusively showed that Jesus Christ is the God of the Bible. Jesus Christ is the Alpha and the Omega. Jesus Christ is the beginning and the end.

Easter for me is significant for the future because it is a conclusive evidence for the deity of Jesus Christ.

And because Jesus Christ is God, He is all-powerful, all-knowing, and all-seeing. Jesus Christ is the Creator of the World who has the world in His hands.

Easter Remembered

Whenever I think about Easter, I remember that hymn, "He's Got the Whole World in His Hands." Easter reminds me that my God Jesus Christ owns this world.

Easter, therefore, gives me hope for the future. I know that Jesus Christ not only has the whole world in His hands, but my whole life. I know that the Lord God Jesus Christ will not let even a strand of my hair fall to the ground, if it is not His will.

I have confidence that my Savior lives. When I think about Easter, I feel like singing, "Because He Lives, I Can Smile Tomorrow." Easter is about hope and promise.

The fact that Jesus Christ died on the cross was to bring me spiritual salvation and give me eternal life. The fact that Jesus Christ rose from the death proved that He is master over sin and death. Jesus Christ rules over even Satan and his evil forces.

I know I can look forward to tomorrow because Jesus Christ is my Savior God.

Easter is the proof that I have eternal life. How wonderful it will be on that day when I enter into eternal life in the Kingdom of Heaven. I, like every other human being on earth,

Easter Remembered

was headed toward eternal damnation and suffering in Hell, where evil beings and Satan dwell for eternity. But Jesus Christ saved me from that wretched eternal death.

Yes, Jesus paid it all, and all to Him I owe. I belong to Jesus Christ for eternity to be in His presence in the Kingdom of Heaven with heavenly angels and those who have also been redeemed by the blood of Jesus Christ, the Savior God.

Easter causes my heart to shout in joy at the hope of life-everlasting. It is eternal life bought with the precious blood of God who took on human flesh to give me eternal life.

No one has done anything close to that extent of love for me. Jesus Christ has. He is God. That is higher than any status this world can confer.

Jesus Christ could have remained in His heavenly realms and let me go to my eternal damnation. But no. Jesus Christ took on human flesh, in order to save me. Jesus Christ loves me that much.

Easter reminds me of the love of Jesus Christ. Jesus Christ loves me so much that He came to this earth and died for me. Jesus

Christ loves me so much that He rose from death for me. Jesus Christ loves me so much that He has extended to me the promise of eternal salvation.

Jesus Christ's love for me is eternal. The love of Jesus Christ cannot be compared with anything else in this world. All the love in this world is ephemeral; they all end at some point.

Even a husband who loves his wife with all that he has and all that he is will eventually die. The wife who is loved to the fullest human potential will be left alone. Even the husband who loves with true love betrays his wife in the final end of his life. When he dies, he leaves his wife alone and sad.

The wife who has been so well-loved will feel tremendous pain and suffering on this earth after her husband dies because she knows what she is missing. When her husband was alive, there was a buffer of great love. But when her husband dies, that loving bubble is burst.

The wife who was loved will feel more lonely than someone who was not well-loved. The wife who was so well-loved will miss the love and miss her husband. But her husband is dead. He has left her for

Easter Remembered

good, never to return again. The husband, who by earthly standards is perfect in love, betrays his wife in the final act of his human existence. His death is betrayal. His death is the ultimate curse, perhaps worse than any tragedy or sadness the wife who was loved has ever experienced in her life.

And this is the case the other way around. A wife who loves her husband with her all betrays her husband in the final act of her life. Her death itself is betrayal. Her death itself is the greatest pain that any person could ever inflect on her husband who was so well loved.

With Jesus Christ, it is completely different. Jesus Christ will never leave me. Jesus Christ is God. He is the Risen Savior, who will never die again. Jesus Christ will always be there.

Jesus Christ, my God, will be there for me during my sickness and health. Jesus Christ, my God, will be there in my moments of strengths as well as my moments of weakness. Jesus Christ, my God, will be there when I am wealthy or when I am poor. Jesus Christ, my God, will be there when I am popular and even when I am hated. Jesus Christ, my God, will stand by me when I am surrounded by loved ones or when I am alone. Jesus Christ will always be there for me.

Jesus Christ is eternal love. Jesus Christ, my God, will be there for me when I am alive or when I am dead. When I die, I will join the eternal presence of Jesus Christ in the Kingdom of Christ. Jesus Christ will be there for me for all eternity.

That is the promise of Easter. That is the hope of Easter. For me, Easter is so much more than Easter egg-hunts and the Easter Bunny. For me, Easter is about a concrete, real love that Jesus Christ has for me that will never fade or die. Jesus Christ will always love me with eternal intensity. Jesus Christ loves me with constant love that is always there for me, in life and in physical death.

There is absolutely no one on earth who will be completely true in love. Even the most loving husband betrays his wife in the reality of his death. There is only one in the whole world who is completely true in love. That is Jesus Christ, my God.

I thank God that in grace I was rescued. I was rescued from my own delusions of grandeur. I was rescued from the fleeting love that I thought I had found comfort in this world. I was rescued from the deception and lies that I thought had made me happy, but which really did not. It was in Jesus Christ, my God, that I found salvation and true, eternal love.

I thought I was relatively happy in life. But a series of events struck. Friends whom I thought were my friend deserted me over some trifling little thing. The "wealth" that I thought I had was almost reduced to nothing in relative terms. The power and authority that I thought I commanded came to naught. I realized that I was not as important as I had previously thought.

Throughout series of events and personal setbacks, I realized that nothing that I had was really secure. As I experienced betrayals and lack of loyalty from my friends, I realized that even my most treasured relationships were not dependable. I realized there was no one I could completely trust.

As I faced the reality of the frailty of humanity that I am a part of, I realized I needed something more. I understood that I need to put my trust in something greater than

Easter Remembered

myself and the world that I thought I had created for myself.

I realized that I needed God. That is when I opened up the Bible and started reading the Good News. The Gospel of Jesus Christ in the New Testament showed me the love of God. Jesus Christ who is God (called, "the Word," in the Gospel of John) came down to this earth and took human flesh to show love to humanity. Therefore, all who believe in Christ Jesus as God will not perish but have eternal life.

When I realized the truth of the Bible, I kneeled and prayed to Jesus Christ to save me from my sins. I asked Jesus Christ to make me His own and love me forever as my God. I told Jesus Christ in prayer that I want to be a child of God, a child of the Promise.

As soon as I prayed in sincerity and earnestness, Jesus Christ gave me deep, spiritual assurance. I felt the presence of Jesus Christ in my heart. I realized that Jesus Christ loved me with an eternal love that would not change regardless of what happened.

I knew in my heart that Jesus Christ will guide me through thick and thin. I understood that I was a recipient of the eternal love of Jesus

Christ. I knew that I would be loved by Jesus Christ, my God, in this life and the next. I knew that I would be loved forever.

Easter, to me, is the promise of the eternal love of Jesus Christ. Every time I celebrate Easter, I am reassured yet again that the love Jesus Christ has for me will never disappear.

I know that I will live forever in the Kingdom of Heaven with Jesus Christ. And this gives me hope in life and hope in death.

For me, Easter is about hope for the future. But my future hope is not limited to my eternal life in Kingdom of Heaven after my death. Easter gives me hope for my future in this world as well.

I know that my God who has conquered death in resurrection will guide me through the troubled waters of this life. There is so much pain and suffering in this world.

The most recent tragedy was the Tsunami disaster in Asia. Many people died. Many people were left homeless. Many people face outbreak of disease.

There are other fears as well. There is the perpetual fear of global terrorism that Americans have to live with. A terrorist bomb can strike anytime and at anywhere. There is really no place that's really safe. And who knows? There may be a nuclear terrorist attack in the future. Life is uncertain.

But with all the pain, death, destruction, and fear around me, I know that Jesus Christ will guide me through the difficulties because I have decided to make Jesus Christ the King of my life.

Those who reject Jesus Christ as the supreme ruler of their lives probably are like me before I accepted Jesus Christ as God. They live in constant fear and uncertainty. I was that way before I accepted Jesus Christ as my Savior God.

But because I have accepted Jesus Christ as my Savior God, I know that Jesus Christ will protect me from all dangers and harm, if that is His will.

Even if I meet danger and harm, I know that Jesus Christ will be with me and will give me the strength to carry on in life as a Christian.

Jesus Christ will love me and comfort me whatever happens. Whatever troubles assail me, whatever destruction stares me in the face, I know that Jesus Christ is in my corner and is walking with me. I know that Jesus Christ will carry me through all difficulties.

The knowledge that Jesus Christ is with me gives me the strength to tackle all difficulties and troubles. The fact of Easter and the evidence for the supreme authority of Jesus give me comfort in my most difficult moments.

If it is His will, Jesus Christ, my God, will drive away my problems. Or if, as in the case of Job, it is God's will for me to endure suffering, I know Jesus Christ will give me the strength to go through the trial. I have true hope in Jesus Christ, my God.

I know Jesus Christ will never leave me or forsake me. Jesus Christ will always be there for me in the Kingdom of Heaven as well as this life on earth.

Easter gives me confidence to live this life on earth. It is great to be a Christian with Easter hope in her heart.

I know that there is no mountain too difficult to climb. I know that there is no fear in death. I know that Jesus Christ is God – the King of kings and the LORD of lords in the whole-wide world.

Easter Remembered

And I can only offer thanks to Jesus Christ for who He is. And I will grab onto the hope of Easter. Easter is the hope for my future.

Easter can be the hope of your future as well if you accept Jesus Christ as God and your Redeemer.

Easter Remembered

"Joy of Easter"

What joy!
What happiness!
Jesus Christ is alive.
Jesus Christ reigns from above.
Jesus Christ is God.

What joy!
What happiness!
Easter fills with hope.
Easter gives peace.
In Easter, I will find my future.

What joy!
What happiness!
Jesus Christ is my God.
Promise of Easter is mine.
I will be raised to eternal life.

What joy!
What happiness!
Jesus Christ is coming back.
Easter assures us of the miracle.
I will be forever with my God.

Easter Remembered

"Jesus Is Arisen!"

From the tomb,
Death and destruction,
Jesus is arisen
To rule the world.

From the depths,
Where worms and decay lie,
Jesus is arisen
To conquer death and sin.

From the shoal,
A place of evil rule,
Jesus is arisen
To prove he is the supreme ruler.

From Hell,
Eternal place of suffering,
Jesus is arisen
To His rightful place in Heaven.

From the cave,
Blocked by rock and unbelief,
Jesus is arisen
To call the faithful to Him.

From death,
The destiny of humankind,
Jesus is arisen
As God everlasting.

Easter Remembered

"Death Not Be Proud"

Death not be proud
That you have put Christ
In the cave of death.

Don't you know?
Christ has risen from death.
The tomb is empty.

Death not be proud
Because Christ was buried
Along with criminals.

Don't you know?
Christ is out and about, alive –
Ruling as the King of the World.

Death not be proud
In the suffering of Jesus
Which preceded his demise.

Don't you know?
Christ conquered suffering
And will comfort His faithful.

Death not be proud
In the knowledge of betrayal
That followed Jesus to the grave.

Easter Remembered

Don't you know?
Christ's disciples multiplied
In the knowledge of the Resurrection.

Death not be proud
To proclaim Jesus' death
As final and decisive.

Don't you know?
Three days later
Jesus proclaimed his victory.

Easter Remembered

"Master of Life"

He is the master of life,
The Lord Jesus Christ,
God everlasting,
The Creator of the World.

In the beginning,
The Word created the world –
All living owe their beginning
To Jesus Christ.

From the slithering life forms,
Crawling on their belly,
To four-legged walking creatures,
And those who run on two feet –

All life forms owe their beginning
To the creative power of the Word,
The Son of God,
The Alpha and the Omega.

Where would the world be
Without the creative energy
The Word of God put into motion
When the world was void?

He is the master of life,
The one who rose from death,
And showed that He lives
And gives life.

Easter Remembered

"The Resurrection"

The Resurrection
Shocked
Like a thunderbolt from the sky.

They looked in bewilderment
At the empty tomb –
The dead body no longer there.

Jesus has risen from the dead,
You see.
He is the Resurrection.

The Resurrection
Awaits
Those who follow Jesus Christ.

There will be eternal life waiting
And all Christians, true believers,
Have a place in Heaven awaiting.

Christians will rise to life
With a new, non-perishable body
To live eternally with Christ.

Easter Remembered

"Life Source"

Jesus is the Life Source,
From where all life flows,
Without whom nothing lives.

Jesus is the Life Source,
To which all life flows,
For energy and maintenance.

Jesus is the Life Source,
Who created the Heavens
And the Earth and all in it.

Jesus is the Life Source,
Where death has no foothold
And destruction is powerless.

Jesus is the Life Source
That regenerates
And makes humans born again.

Jesus is the Life Source –
The source of resurrection
And new life.

Jesus is the Life Source;
For, without Him,
There is no life.

Easter Remembered

"Give Me Life"

Give me life,
Lord Jesus Christ.
I know you own life.

There is death and destruction.
Life is uncertain.
Evil men seek to dominate.

Terrorists prowl like a lion
Trying to devour innocent lambs.
Death lurks everywhere.

Snares are set
For the good of the earth
Who want to serve you.

But you are the master of life.
Give me life
In this world and next.

I know you alone can.
You created life
And you sustain life.

Give me life
To serve you
And to glorify you.

Easter Remembered

"Future Hope"

Future hope,
That's what you are,
God Jesus Christ;
For, you have conquered death.

Resurrected,
You are the God of life,
Lord of all living things –
You are the Creator God.

My heart will hope in you,
The Future Hope.
You have redeemed me,
And you will guide me.

What will I hope in,
But in you Jesus Christ?
Even in the darkest moments,
You are my future hope.

Even when my enemies assail me,
I will trust in you, Jesus Christ,
Because you are the Resurrection
And the Life Eternal.

You are my future hope,
Savior and Master of my life,
Jesus Christ.
You are my God.

Easter Remembered

"Jesus Is My God"

Jesus is my God.
What is His name?
Christ,
Messiah,
Immanuel.

He has many names
And many titles,
But He is the same
God the Son –

A part of the Triune God
The Bible teaches –
Defended for thousands of years
By deep Christian piety.

Jesus is my God
And I will serve Him
As King of kings
And the LORD of lords.

Jesus will return to judge
The quick and the dead.
As He was resurrected from death,
So shall His followers in the last day.

Jesus is My God
Who will give me new life
For life eternal
To rule with Him.

Easter Remembered

"Divine Power"

Who can boast of divine power,
But Jesus Christ the LORD?
For He alone is God –
There is none beside Him.

No earthly power can wax in pride
And scoff at the Name of the Word.
Jesus Christ reigns supreme
As the Creator and Sustainer.

He is the life and resurrection,
Jesus Christ who rose from death.
God the Son conquered death
And the evil forces of Satan.

No grave has the power to hold Him.
No rock can block the exit to life.
No guards can keep Him down.
No demon has hold on Him.

Divine Power,
The property of God the Son,
Reigns and silences
The foes of the Bible truth.

Jesus Christ reigns
With divine hosts
And the forces of the created order
From everlasting to everlasting.

Easter Remembered

"The Judge"

Jesus sits as the Judge
At the right hand of God the Father.
Mighty angels attend Him,
And saints honor him with hymns.

He who was mocked,
Spat at,
Taunted in mock trial
Now stands as the Judge.

The innocent one
Who suffered abuse
For no good reason
Will deliver the verdict.

Jewish religious leaders
Tricked, connived, and paid
To have Him killed,
Corrupting the arm of justice.

But He is exalted as the Judge,
Jesus Christ is His name,
The one who will return
To judge the quick and the dead.

Who can deny Jesus Christ
His role as the Judge
Passing sentence over all –
To Heaven or to Hell.

Easter Remembered

"The Disciples"

Where are all the disciples?
Where have the students gone?
The ones who learned from Christ
Are nowhere to be seen.

They have run away
Like chicken without their heads,
Running this way and that
With no purpose in the world.

They have fled
Out of fear
In trepidation
As evil forces closed in.

Jesus' followers
Escaped their capture
Rather than stand by with Christ
To suffer with Him.

Where are they all?
The disciples of Christ
For whom Christ gave His all
Have disappeared like flies.

On the day of Resurrection,
The first Easter,
Jesus' 12 disciples
Were nowhere to be seen.

Easter Remembered

"The Women"

The women were there
While the twelve were not seen.
They visited the tomb of Christ
Early on Easter Sunday.

Where were the tough men
Who bragged
And once stood tall
Next to the Son of Man?

They had fled in fear
As Christ was arrested,
Taunted in a mock trial,
And nailed to the cross.

The women remained.
Sure, they were afraid.
Who would not be?
But they remained.

The women visited the tomb.
They were blessed;
For, they were the first
To witness the Resurrection.

Perceived to be frail,
Socially weak
Without political power,
The women stood upright.

Easter Remembered

"Glory"

Glory to the Risen One,
Jesus Christ the LORD,
The Creator of the World.

Glory to the Resurrected,
God who conquers death,
Who will judge all humans.

Glory to the Conqueror,
Who vanquished his enemies,
Those who oppose His rule.

Glory to the Creator,
Who has created the world
And will recreate it in the end.

Glory to the Savior,
Who died on the cross
And brought me salvation.

Glory to the Almighty,
The Lord of history
And of the future.

About the Author

Maria Alvarez is happy to be a Christian, living in America. Alvarez has experienced Easter joy and relies in the hope of Resurrection. And Alvarez likes to share her Easter joy with everyone she meets.

http://www.TheHermitKingdomPress.com

www.ingramcontent.com/pod-product-compliance
Lightning Source LLC
Chambersburg PA
CBHW020015050426
42450CB00005B/483